ORCA
FOOTPRINT

Get Outside!

HOW HUMANS CONNECT WITH NATURE

LEAH PAYNE

ORCA BOOK PUBLISHERS

Published in Canada and the United States in 2024 by Orca Book Publishers.
orcabook.com

Library and Archives Canada Cataloguing in Publication
Title: Get outside! : how humans connect with nature / Leah Payne.
Names: Payne, Leah (Leah S.), author.
Series: Orca footprints.
Description: Series statement: Orca footprints ; 30 |
Includes bibliographical references and index.
Identifiers: Canadiana (print) 20230465447 | Canadiana (ebook) 20230465455 |
ISBN 9781459836877 (hardcover) | ISBN 9781459832091 (PDF) |
ISBN 9781459832107 (EPUB)
Subjects: LCSH: Human ecology—Juvenile literature.
Classification: LCC GF48 .P39 2024 | DDC j304.2—dc23

Library of Congress Control Number: 2023940294

Summary: Part of the nonfiction Orca Footprints series for middle-grade readers, illustrated with photographs throughout, this book examines the connection between humans and nature, why that connection is important and what we can learn from being outdoors.

Orca Book Publishers is committed to reducing the consumption of nonrenewable resources in the production of our books. We make every effort to use materials that support a sustainable future.

Orca Book Publishers gratefully acknowledges the support for its publishing programs provided by the following agencies: the Government of Canada, the Canada Council for the Arts and the Province of British Columbia through the BC Arts Council and the Book Publishing Tax Credit.

Front cover photos by (top) Alexander Spatari/Getty Images; (bottom) RelaxFoto.de/Getty Images
Back cover photos by (from left) wundervisuals/Getty Images; Klaus Vedfelt/Getty Images; Inti St Clair/Getty Images
Design by Troy Cunningham
Edited by Kirstie Hudson

Printed and bound in South Korea.

27   26   25   24   •   1   2   3   4

For my sister and cousins.
Growing up together and exploring nature with
you was an immense joy and privilege.

Contents

CHAPTER ONE
WHAT IS NATURE, REALLY?

CHAPTER TWO
NATURE IS WONDERFUL...
FOR EVERYONE

CHAPTER THREE
LET'S LEARN FROM NATURE

CHAPTER FOUR
LET'S LIVE WITH NATURE

Introduction

Take a moment to consider how often you interact with nature in your everyday life. This might include playing outside at recess or walking to school.

JOHN M LUND PHOTOGRAPHY INC/GETTY IMAGES

Every day we distance ourselves from nature in many ways. We spend most of our time in buildings that are designed to keep the "outside" out and the "inside" in. We heat and cool our homes, schools and workplaces—and our cars too. We play indoors on our computers or tablets if it's raining outside. We even have indoor playgrounds!

But it didn't used to be that way. People didn't always see themselves as separate from the natural world. And it's still not that way in many places around the globe and in many different cultures. Scientific research tells us that having a close relationship with nature can help us be healthier, happier and more likely to take action to help the environment. This isn't surprising. In fact, the connection between all living things (including humans) is something that traditional Indigenous wisdom has long recognized.

The natural world has so much to teach us! How can we improve our relationship with "the great outdoors" and make sure that all

people have equal access to nature? In the following chapters, we'll explore different ways in which we can become closer to nature and improve our lives, buildings and communities in the process. We'll also be meeting some amazing people who are working to deepen our connection to the outside world. Together we can learn how to nurture nature, and how to let it nurture us.

A learning experience can be had each and every time we head outdoors. Consider asking your grandparents or other elders in your life to share some of their knowledge and wisdom about the natural world.

What Is Nature, Really?

G et out your magnifying glass! It's time to be a detective and ask questions. What is nature anyway? Are humans part of it or separate from it? Do all people think about and relate to nature in the same way? Let's find out!

US VERSUS NATURE

There really isn't one perfect definition of nature. Sure, it includes waterfalls and meadows, flowers and trees, rocks and animals. But does nature also include a city park? What about a lone dandelion peeking out through cracks in the sidewalk? Or a houseplant? Or a house cat? And what about us—are we part of nature? It depends *who* you ask and also *when* you ask them. Our views of ourselves and our relationship with nature aren't set— they change as our societies change.

Peekaboo! Nature is all around us. The trick is slowing down and taking the time to notice it.
FLAVIO COELHO/GETTY IMAGES

For example, if we look back in time to the *Age of Enlightenment* (which happened in Europe in the 17th and 18th centuries), people and nature were thought of as separate. Part of the Enlightenment movement (which valued rational thought and science) was the belief that people can (and should) dominate nature. Later on, the *Industrial Revolution* (which happened in Europe and North America in the 18th and 19th centuries) created a huge shift in society from farming to manufacturing. This movement saw nature as *resources* to be taken and used by humans while it also created pollution and caused habitat destruction.

Both of these movements continue to affect our values and way of life. Many people today still tend to think of themselves as separate from nature in many ways. (Sometimes we even use the term *natural* to mean anything that humans haven't created!) And, unfortunately, we still create wide-scale pollution and habitat destruction.

Do you have a beautiful stream near your home like these kids do? Your natural landscape will look different depending on where you live. Perhaps you have forests and meadows, or maybe you have city parks and gardens.
INTI ST CLAIR/GETTY IMAGES

The Industrial Revolution brought about the massive rise of factories. In addition to pollution, this led to poor working conditions and child labor.
ALEXANDROS MARAGOS/GETTY IMAGES

When we talk about protecting nature, we sometimes forget that protecting nature is also protecting *ourselves*. Protecting **pollinators**, for example, is vitally important for humans. An estimated 100 crops provide 90 percent of the food we eat, and more than 70 of these crops are pollinated by bees, according to the United Nations Environment Program. People really are part of the natural world.

WHERE DID ALL THE NATURE GO?

Cities have existed for thousands of years. Until relatively recently, though, most people lived in **rural** areas, with plenty of nature around them. But during the Industrial Revolution, more and more people moved to **urban** areas to find jobs in factories instead of on farms. Today almost 60 percent of the world's population lives in cities. In Canada that number rises to almost 74 percent, and in the United States it's even higher—around 83 percent of people live in cities. Researchers estimate that by 2050, 7 out of 10 people around the globe will live in cities.

Nature certainly can—and does!—exist in cities. (We'll touch on that more in chapters 2 and 3.) It includes things like trees, ponds and urban animals, of course, but there are other types of nature, like the night sky and natural sounds, which are under threat from pollution.

Light pollution is excessive or inappropriate use of outdoor artificial light at nighttime, when it's naturally dark outside. Caused by streetlights, lights on buildings, lit-up signs and advertisements and even light from

Have you ever flown in an airplane at night? If so, you might have stared in awe at the lights down below in the cities. What you were looking at is known as light pollution.
DENNISVDW/GETTY IMAGES

boats, light pollution is a big problem. It affects human health and disrupts animal behavior. It can confuse animals trying to migrate by the light of the moon, for example. It harms human health by confusing our natural sleep cycles. Can you see the stars at night in your neighborhood? You may have to travel farther into the countryside for an evening of stargazing.

🍃 ***Noise pollution*** is unwanted and disturbing sound. If you've ever lived near a big construction project or a busy road, you might know how annoying loud noises can be— especially when they go on for a long time. Like light pollution, noise pollution tends to occur in urban areas and can affect animals and people. Noise pollution can also exist outside of cities, such as when ships in the ocean emit noise that interferes with communication between whales.

In addition to harming our hearing, noise pollution can cause stress, sleep disturbances and high blood pressure.
FOTOG/GETTY IMAGES

The night sky and natural sounds don't technically go anywhere, of course. Even in cities, they still exist. But human activity makes it harder for us to see, hear and appreciate nature.

DO WE HAVE A NATURE DEFICIT?

How much time do you spend in nature every week? Young people today spend less time playing outside than previous generations did. Reasons for this include more scheduled activities (like after-school lessons) and more screen time (like video games). But it's not just kids— adults also spend less time in nature than their parents or grandparents did. It's a phenomenon that American author Richard Louv calls ***nature-deficit disorder***. He believes our society is moving toward more and more time inside, away from nature. Because of that, most of us are disconnected from the natural world.

Scientists measure sound in decibels. A soft whisper, for example, is 30 decibels. Gas-powered leaf blowers can be 85 decibels, and the siren from an emergency vehicle, 120. If we are exposed to loud noises for too long, we can damage our hearing.

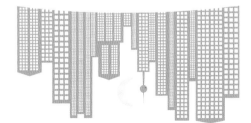

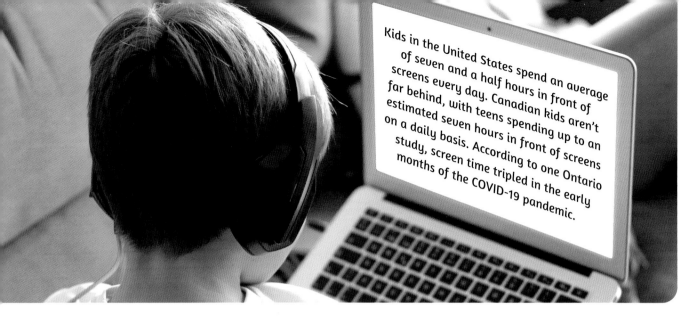

Kids in the United States spend an average of seven and a half hours in front of screens every day. Canadian kids aren't far behind, with teens spending up to an estimated seven hours in front of screens on a daily basis. According to one Ontario study, screen time tripled in the early months of the COVID-19 pandemic.

ISABEL PAVIA/GETTY IMAGES

As part of his role as Elders and Indigenous Knowledge Facilitator, John Harris supports land-based education for students.

CHRIS COURCHENE

NUTS'A'MAAT

It's important to understand that the concept of humans being disconnected from nature is not universal. It hasn't been the case throughout history, and it's not the case in many places around the world today. For example, many Indigenous Peoples consider humans a part of nature and have a long tradition of respecting and protecting the environment. Knowledge often comes from the experiences had by people observing and interacting with nature, and this knowledge is then passed down from generation to generation.

John Harris is the Elders and Indigenous Knowledge Facilitator for the Greater Victoria School District in British Columbia. He is from the Snuneymuxw First Nation, whose Traditional Territory is located along the Pacific Northwest coast of Canada, near present-day Nanaimo, British Columbia. Harris uses the term *nuts'a'maat* (which is a word from the Hul'q'umi'num' language) to describe the interconnectedness of all living things and to remind us that we are all one.

Rather than believing that there is a hierarchy of living things (with humans at the top, animals in the middle and plants at the bottom), Snuneymuxw First Nation culture teaches that humans are a part of nature and that every living thing matters and should be treated with respect. Nuts'a'maat is a reminder to take only what we need and be responsible caretakers of the land. For example, it's important, as a sign of respect, to give thanks to a tree when we use its bark or roots and to not take from nature without giving back. The concept teaches us that what happens in nature affects humans too because we are all interconnected. This means that helping to heal the environment is healing to ourselves too.

We Are the Land

We can look at ancient clam gardens as an example. First Nations living along the Pacific Northwest coast have carefully and skillfully tended these habitats for thousands of years. Managing these gardens helped clams thrive, provided people with a healthy and sustainable food source and helped support other tidal species too. Recent clam-garden restoration projects are helping clams thrive again. These projects are also wonderful ways for Indigenous community members to participate in traditional **mariculture**, which creates space to revitalize their cultural food practices.

Harris explains that his personal connection to the land developed during his childhood, when his dad would take him out hunting and fishing and teach him all about the world around them. It was the way his dad had been raised, and now Harris does the same with his own children. "I grew up learning that we *are* the land, and we are *from* the land," he says. "Whenever we were out for a walk, my dad would talk about the plants and trees around us." This deep respect for the environment is built into the culture and language of the Snuneymuxw First Nation. Harris explains that he prefers to talk about what a plant gives us rather than what we can use it for.

FRILUFTSLIV

In Nordic countries (such as Sweden, Norway, Denmark and Finland) people have a strong connection to nature. It even has its

Shinrin-yoku is a Japanese term that translates into English as "forest bathing." It refers to the calming and restorative act of spending time in the forest and taking in its atmosphere. Anyone can enjoy forest bathing. The next time you're in the forest, slow down and use your senses to take in the sights and smells and sounds around you.
MINT IMAGES/GETTY IMAGES

John Harris encourages us all to act as good caretakers of the land and get involved in projects like litter cleanups and **nature-restoration** work. He also invites young people to develop relationships with their local communities. For example, you could attend events that are open to the public, like Orange Shirt Day events. It's equally important to learn more about Indigenous Peoples in our communities, so we better understand the complex history and present-day relationships we have with Indigenous Peoples in Canada and the United States. Finally he urges young people to connect with elders in their own lives, who have wisdom to share and support to give.

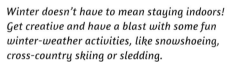

Winter doesn't have to mean staying indoors! Get creative and have a blast with some fun winter-weather activities, like snowshoeing, cross-country skiing or sledding.
GOLERO/GETTY IMAGES

own name—*friluftsliv* (pronounced free-loofts-liv). Friluftsliv means "open-air living." It's a way of life that prioritizes and revolves around time spent in nature. Fresh air is seen as healthy and important for everyone, including very young children. Even babies nap in their strollers outside in the winter (bundled in their cozy clothes).

Linda Åkeson McGurk is a Swedish American journalist, author and mom. The title of her first book, *There's No Such Thing as Bad Weather*, refers to a Nordic expression that translates in English as "There's no such thing as bad weather, just bad clothes." Why? Well, when it's cold, rainy or snowy (as it often is in Nordic countries), kids and adults dress for the weather and spend time outside.

"I think we have a very special bond with nature," McGurk explains. "We are raised to honor nature and to know that we are a part of nature. This 'oneness' with nature is really important, so we don't see nature as something separate from ourselves. Humans and nature are one." Like the Coast Salish idea of nuts'a'maat, this close relationship can help remind people that nature isn't just a series of resources that humans can take and that what we do to nature impacts what happens to us.

McGurk describes how this emotional bond with nature can be combined with education to promote environmentalism. In Scandinavia tales of magical trolls help teach conservation and **environmental stewardship** to kids. The troll characters are even used in preschool classrooms to help teach children to protect the environment, such as by not littering.

TIME TO REFLECT

Nuts'a'maat and friluftsliv are two examples of meaningful concepts that help us connect with nature. John Harris encourages all of us to reflect on our own understandings of how we relate to the land. Our relationship with nature can be informed by our families, our languages, our cultures and our backgrounds.

Consider asking your grandparents or other elders in your life how they value nature, or ask them about some of their traditional practices and beliefs. With the help of an adult, you can also do research online or visit a cultural center for more insight. Taking time to explore our cultures and ask important questions can help us find meaning and feel a connection with our ancestors. Doing so can also remind us of all the ways we can continue to celebrate, cherish and give thanks to the nature around us every day.

NATURE SPOTLIGHT: *Friluftsliv in Our Daily Lives*
Here are some suggestions from Linda Åkeson McGurk on how we can practice friluftsliv.

- Walk places whenever we can, rather than taking the bus or getting a ride.

- Observe how the seasons change where we live, such as looking for tadpoles or birds that have come home from their annual migrations.

- Take some of your indoor activities outdoors and make them part of your daily routine, such as doing your homework outside.

- Learn practical outdoor skills, such as fire-starting (safely, with adult supervision).

- Enjoy nature with friends—have a picnic lunch, for example.

- Dress in comfortable, weather-appropriate clothes so you can enjoy your time outside.

- Cook and eat outside as a family. Everyone can have a job, whether it's grilling or chopping veggies.

CHAPTER TWO

Nature Is Wonderful... for Everyone

What's so great about nature anyway? Does everyone get to enjoy nature in the same way? In this chapter we will explore the many benefits of nature. We'll also discuss problems, like why access to nature isn't equal for everyone and how racialized people have been excluded from outdoor recreation. We'll talk about how we can make nature inclusive for everyone, because nature *is* meant for everyone.

WHY IS TIME IN NATURE IMPORTANT?

It's a bit of a silly question, isn't it? How exactly do you measure something that is part of what makes us human? Research shows us that nature is a key part of our health and happiness.

We all have a responsibility to learn the history of the land on which we live, work and play. This includes learning more about the Indigenous Peoples who first lived there—and who still live there today. Using online tools such as native-land.ca is a good place to start.
THOMAS BARWICK/GETTY IMAGES

According to scientific studies, spending time outdoors in nature is associated with:

- reduced stress and less anxiety
- a more positive mood
- improved attention, concentration and memory
- a sense of meaningfulness
- feelings of joy and calmness
- better mental health later in life
- more physical activity
- healthy eyesight

It doesn't end there! Research also shows that spending lots of time in nature as kids might make us want to spend more time in **green spaces** as adults. Plus, research shows that people are more inclined to try to protect the environment if they spent lots of time in nature as kids. Fostering our connection with nature might even help us cope with the worry and sadness that can come when we learn about environmental problems such as **climate change** and plastic pollution.

In an effort to spend more time in nature, some families try to track their time outside. There's even an initiative called 1000 Hours Outside, which encourages people to try to spend 1,000 hours outdoors every year—that's almost three hours outside each day.
KLAUS VEDFELT/GETTY IMAGES

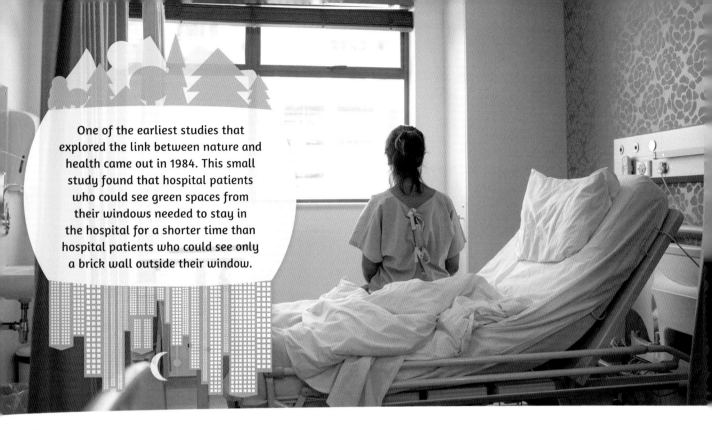

One of the earliest studies that explored the link between nature and health came out in 1984. This small study found that hospital patients who could see green spaces from their windows needed to stay in the hospital for a shorter time than hospital patients who could see only a brick wall outside their window.

STÍGUR MÁR KARLSSON/
HEIMSMYNDIR/GETTY IMAGES

THE BENEFITS OF URBAN NATURE

Spending our free time in nature is great, but it's not the only way we interact with the natural world, of course. The truth is, nature is all around us all the time, even if we live in the middle of a city. People in cities share space with animals like raccoons and pigeons, tend community gardens that grow food, and live on streets lined with trees. Next time you're in the city, consider the nature that might be hiding in plain sight!

Just like the wilderness, urban nature can bring huge bene-fits to us. For example, city trees can:

- provide *tree canopy* and reduce heat (by providing shade and helping to cool streets)
- act as shelter and food for animals like squirrels and birds
- reduce air pollution and clean the air
- help prevent flooding
- protect *biodiversity*

Urban gardens can:

- increase access to fresh, healthy food
- reduce food costs for nearby families
- promote community relationships and friendship
- encourage physical activity (gardening is hard work!)
- improve mental health and well-being

Does your city or town allow community gardens? Check out your municipality's website for more information on how to get involved.
BRUCE YUANYUE BI/GETTY IMAGES

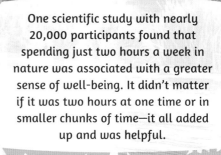

One scientific study with nearly 20,000 participants found that spending just two hours a week in nature was associated with a greater sense of well-being. It didn't matter if it was two hours at one time or in smaller chunks of time—it all added up and was helpful.

19

Note how many trees, bushes and flowers are growing on this city street. When it's hot, green spaces help cool us down.
MITCH DIAMOND/GETTY IMAGES

WHO 'BELONGS' IN NATURE?

Everyone belongs in nature, of course! All people (grown-ups and kids of all ages and abilities) should be able to enjoy the outdoors equally and experience its endless joys. Unfortunately, that's not always the case. Scientific research shows us why being in nature is important and also who might be missing out. Scientists ask questions like, Where are green spaces in urban areas, and who gets access to them? Which neighborhoods have more trees than others, and why? Most important, how can we fix things so everyone gets to enjoy nature equally?

A study in 2020 found that American children living in poverty have less access to parks. Another study from the United States found that in 92 percent of urban areas included in the study, low-income areas had less tree cover than high-income areas. **Tree inequity** is a term for the reality that some neighborhoods have fewer trees than others. As we learned earlier in this chapter, this can have health and environmental consequences.

Low-income areas in the study were an average of 2.7ºF (1.5ºC) hotter because there is less tree cover. Some areas were an incredible 7.2ºF (4ºC) hotter! This can make a huge difference on scorching summer days. The pattern is similar in Canada. Racialized groups also have less access to green space. (We'll discuss this more in chapter 3.)

Many cities have plans to plant more trees. For example, Vancouver, BC, has committed to increasing the number of trees in many low-income neighborhoods by the year 2030.

Note the absence of trees, bushes and other plants on this city street. Urban areas without green spaces tend to get hotter in warm weather.
PGIAM/GETTY IMAGES

INCLUSIVE OUTDOORS

Inequity also exists in who gets to enjoy natural spaces comfortably and safely. If we travel far enough back in time, we can see that this is not a new idea at all. The beginnings of the ***conservation movement*** in North America were rooted in racism. Many celebrated environmentalists of the 1800s and 1900s wanted to "conserve" the wilderness for white people to enjoy. For example,

Birding can be a wonderful activity. To get started, look for a youth birding organization near you. You can also get involved in a project like the Great Backyard Bird Count.
FUSE/GETTY IMAGES

between 1890 and 1920, the Stoney Nakoda people were forcibly removed from Alberta's Banff National Park, which was part of their Traditional Lands. George Stewart, the park superintendent, thought that all Indigenous Peoples should be banned from their traditional hunting areas in the new park.

This is an example of ***environmental racism***—discrimination in environmental policies and decision-making based on race. Sadly, environmental racism still exists today. In New York City's Central Park in May 2020, Amy Cooper (a white woman) called 911 to falsely report that Christian Cooper (a Black male ***birder***) was threatening her life, after he asked her to leash her dog. Black birders and nature enthusiasts noted that this well-known incident is just one example in a pattern of racist incidents that occur when they try to enjoy time in nature.

Black Birders Week was created in response to the Central Park birdwatching incident. It highlights Black birders and nature enthusiasts. It also brings attention to the inequitable treatment that Black people receive outdoors.

Visual Representation

The outdoor industry has been criticized over the years for its historic lack of diversity in advertising. For example, one study from 2004 examined more than 4,000 ads from three different magazines from 1984 to 2000. The researchers found that the ads rarely showed Black people in an outdoor environment or taking part in outdoor recreation activities. Instead, Black people were typically shown in urban or suburban settings.

All around the world, activists and organizations are working to change that. Judith Kasiama created the organization Colour the Trails to advocate for inclusive representation in outdoor spaces. Kasiama is a Congolese Canadian who loves traveling and adventuring in nature. In 2018 she called out the former prominent

Canadian outdoor company Mountain Equipment Co-op (MEC) for its lack of diversity in advertising. Colour the Trails organizes outdoor events and activities for Black, Indigenous, and other People of Color. These events and activities are accessible and introductory, so participants can learn new skills (like kayaking or mountain biking) in a safe, fun and inclusive environment. "We want to reclaim the outdoors," Kasiama says. She encourages everyone, including young people, to be curious and try out new activities and hobbies.

In addition to creating events, Kasiama explains, Colour the Trails works with local and national parks systems "to ensure that everyone feels safe visiting our parks systems." She also works with brands and businesses to make sure they are inclusive, with diverse imagery and storytelling. "Role models define what is possible," she says.

Colour the Trails founder Judith Kasiama loves adventuring outside.
PAVEL BOIKO

BE AN INTERSECTIONAL ENVIRONMENTALIST

Have a great idea for incorporating intersectional environmentalism into your community? Feeling inspired to make the outdoors more inclusive? Consider chatting with your teacher to create a class project about the topic.
SLADIC/GETTY IMAGES

We can all help! One of the ways we can help make sure that nature is inclusive for everyone is to practice **intersectional environmentalism**. It's a term first used by activist Leah Thomas in 2020. It means that we can't examine environmental issues without also examining social issues (like how race, class and gender come into play and overlap). When we practice intersectional environmentalism, we focus on including historically underrepresented voices. In chapter 4 we'll explore some ways in which we can practice intersectional environmentalism in our everyday lives.

It's important that we work toward a world in which everyone can safely and comfortably enjoy time in nature. This includes people of all ethnicities, genders, sexual orientations, abilities and body shapes and sizes.

Dr. Melissa Lem believes we can all benefit from quality time in nature.
COURTESY OF MELISSA LEM

NATURE SPOTLIGHT: *Nature Prescriptions*

Imagine going to the doctor and getting a prescription to spend more time in nature. This is now a reality for many people, due to the trailblazing work of doctors like Melissa Lem. She was the founding director of PaRx (parkprescriptions.ca), with the BC Parks Foundation. It helps health professionals improve their patients' health by educating them about the benefits of time spent in nature.

As a young person of Chinese descent living in a mostly white area, Lem says she sometimes felt alone, but she found a sense of belonging and connection in nature. Later, when she grew up and became a doctor, she noticed how much more stressed she felt working in the busy city, surrounded

by concrete and glass buildings, compared to when she was working in a rural area, surrounded by nature. This prompted Lem to review scientific studies about the health benefits of nature. What she discovered inspired her to promote time spent in nature as a key pillar of health that can benefit everyone (kids *and* grown-ups).

"There are now four decades of research that describe the benefits of nature for our health," says Lem. And we don't need to make huge changes in our lives to enjoy the benefits of nature, she explains. Meaningful time in nature is what's most important, and we get to determine what is meaningful for us, whether it's gardening in our backyards or spending time in a city park.

Have you visited all the awesome parks near you? Consider making a "bucket list" of green spaces and trails near you to explore.
NOEL HENDRICKSON/GETTY IMAGES

Researchers found that people spent much more time in parks early in the COVID-19 pandemic than they did before the pandemic. It's no wonder why! Being outside is considered lower risk when it comes to the spread of the novel coronavirus, so families were more likely to enjoy activities such as camping, fishing and hiking.

CHAPTER THREE

Let's Learn from Nature

Who knew that the Velcro on every toddler's favorite shoes was inspired by burrs? Paying attention to our surroundings and applying some creative thinking can lead to very cool inventions.
REBECCA DROBIS/GETTY IMAGES

We can all learn from nature. This chapter will share how we can use our relationship with nature to improve the world for individuals, communities and the environment, as well as adapt to the challenges brought about by our changing climate.

NATURE-INSPIRED DESIGN

Many inventions that we use every day are inspired by nature. Modeling an invention after something found in nature is called *biomimicry*. Velcro, for example, was invented by a Swiss engineer named George de Mestral. One day in 1941, he noticed burrs (the small, rough, hooklike parts of certain plants) caught in his dog's fur. The experience inspired him to create the invention we know today as Velcro.

Indigenous Peoples around the world have been applying biomimicry for generations as part of their cultural practices. One example is the winter clothing designed and worn by the Nenets people in Arctic Russia. To stay warm in the extreme cold, people use their knowledge of the land and its animals as inspiration, wearing smartly designed clothing and footwear made from reindeer fur and skin. Reindeer fur consists of a top layer of thick, hollow guard hairs and an undercoat of dense fine hair. This insulation allows reindeer to stay unbothered by the cold and wind in temperatures as low as -79.6°F (-62°C)!

It's no surprise that clothing made from reindeer fur also keeps the wearer warm—it works in the same way. It also keeps the wearer afloat in the water because of the air inside the hollow hairs. In addition, boot soles are made from hide taken from the space between the toes of the reindeer's hooves. This part of the hide is covered with tough, bristlelike fur that helps prevent slipping and keeps snow and ice balls from forming between the reindeer's toes. And, of course, this clothing is also fully biodegradable, so it returns to nature at the end of its life cycle, and there is no waste.

NATURE AND BUILDINGS

Since ancient times buildings have been designed with nature in mind. Strategic design works with nature (rather than against it) to promote efficiency and keep people comfortable. For example, in ancient Egypt and the Persian Empire, "wind catchers" were added to the tops of buildings. They helped trap wind and draw it down into the buildings to keep them and their inhabitants cool in

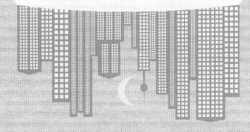

Many medicines we use today were inspired by nature or use ingredients from plants. The common medicine acetylsalicylic acid (known as aspirin) originated from a plant compound found in the bark of white willow trees. Today scientists continue to look to nature to help them discover new medicines.

These ancient "wind catchers" are inspiring current-day scientists to learn how to keep modern buildings cool.
IZZET KERIBAR/GETTY IMAGES

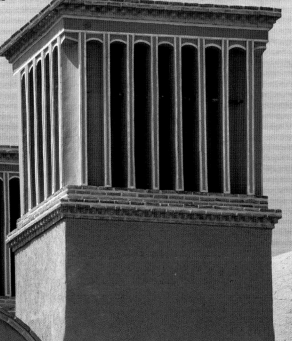

the heat. Compare this to 21st-century glass skyscrapers, which become very hot in the summer because of all the glass and rely on energy-intensive air-conditioning for cooling!

Thankfully, once again people are turning toward nature to improve building design. Creative and sustainable building design uses:

- features that maximize shade to keep people cool
- roofs that catch and use rainwater
- "living walls" and rooftop gardens, parks and green spaces to help reduce heat and improve air quality
- architecture that promotes natural ventilation that keeps people cool and reduces energy costs
- on-site solar panels and wind turbines to create electricity
- lighter-colored buildings and roofs to reflect heat and keep people cool in extreme heat
- windows made from special glass that lets in less heat

NATURE AND COMMUNITIES

It's not just individual buildings that can be designed with nature. Entire communities can be better designed with nature in mind. Communities that incorporate nature can be safer, healthier cities for people *and* the planet.

The *urban heat island effect* refers to how cities tend to trap and intensify heat. Cities can be up to 21.6°F (12°C) hotter than the nearby countryside! Typically the most dense parts of a city are the hottest. That's because tall buildings that are close together block airflow, and dark roads and rooftops absorb radiation from the sun. Being surrounded by surfaces like asphalt can actually make us feel warmer. The heat is made even worse by car engines and indoor air-conditioning, both of which push heat outside and further warm the outdoors. Altogether it's the perfect storm to create extreme heat. And since most of us live in urban areas, the urban heat island effect is a big problem.

Living walls are growing (pun intended!) in popularity. You might spy them inside or outside office buildings, hotels or malls. Some people even create living walls in their homes.

ULTRAFORMA/GETTY IMAGES

Keeping Cool

But the urban heat island effect doesn't affect everyone equally. In chapter 2 we learned that marginalized people are less likely to live in areas with lots of green space nearby. It's no surprise, then, that marginalized groups are more likely to be subjected to extreme heat and less likely to be able to access cooling methods like air-conditioning. A Canadian study from 2022 found that new immigrants and people with low incomes are more likely to live in areas that experience extreme heat.

There are solutions though. During heat waves, cities can adopt strategies like opening "cooling centers," where people can escape the heat, and extending hours for public pools and spray parks. But that's not all—community design matters too. Smart urban planning can actually help *prevent* extreme heat in the first place.

Where buildings are located makes a difference. For example, cities can make use of cool breezes that come off nearby water by avoiding building tall structures close to the water, where they would block breezes. More trees, green space and shade make a big difference too. Some cities are removing asphalt to build nature-filled urban parks and gardens. In New York some rooftops are

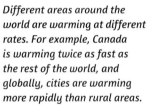

Buildings that meet strict energy-efficient criteria can receive Passive House certification. These eco-friendly buildings can consume up to 90 percent less energy for heating and cooling than conventional buildings. They can be houses but also other types of buildings, like office buildings, schools and supermarkets.

Different areas around the world are warming at different rates. For example, Canada is warming twice as fast as the rest of the world, and globally, cities are warming more rapidly than rural areas.
© MARCO BOTTIGELLI/
GETTY IMAGES

With smart urban planning that incorporates green spaces, spending time outside in the summer heat can be more enjoyable.
NEMKE/GETTY IMAGES

being painted with special coatings that reflect solar heat and UV rays. It's part of a program called New York City Cool Roofs. Creative ideas such as these help make neighborhoods more resilient to climate change and extreme heat.

HARNESSING THE POWER OF NATURE

Nature is powerful, and humans can make use of that power in many creative ways. **Renewable energy** is energy that comes from natural sources that can be replenished by nature faster than they are consumed. (By contrast, **fossil fuels** like oil and natural gas take millions of years to form.) Generating energy from renewable sources creates much lower emissions than burning fossil fuels, so using renewable energy is one of the keys to fighting climate change. Here are some types of renewable energy.

- **Solar power** is energy generated from the sun. Even on cloudy days, solar panels can generate power for things like heating, cooling and electricity.

- **Wind power** is energy generated from moving air. Large turbines that generate wind energy can be on land or even in water, like in the ocean.

- *Hydropower* is energy generated from moving water. Flowing water may be able to be used for drinking water and irrigation as well as for energy.

- *Geothermal energy* is energy generated from heat deep within the earth's core. This heat can be used directly for heating, or steam from the heat can be used to make electricity.

Renewable energy can be used on a large scale, such as providing electricity for cities. Honolulu uses more solar power per capita than any other US city. In fact, Hawaii has committed to using 100 percent renewable energy by 2045. Renewable energy can also be used on a small scale, such as installing solar panels on houses.

Harness the Power of Nature at Home

There are many other ways that we can use the power of nature. Here are some you may be able to do at home with your families or at school with your friends.

- *Collect rainwater.* Ask if your municipality has a rain-barrel program. If they're allowed in your area, you can collect rainwater to help water plants.

- *Grow a garden.* Whether a windowsill herb garden, a container of tomatoes on the balcony or a full vegetable plot in a backyard, gardens are a true testament to how amazing (and powerful) nature is. Plus, you get to eat the final product!

- *Hang your laundry to dry.* Make use of the warmth of the sun by drying your clothes outside in the summertime on a clothesline or drying rack. How's that for solar power?

Extreme heat can be deadly. During British Columbia's 2021 heat dome, for example, temperatures in some regions rose above 104°F (40°C) for days in late June. Six hundred and nineteen people died because of the heat. Most were elderly or vulnerable people who were not able to escape the extreme heat indoors in cities. Research also suggests that a lack of nearby green space may have contributed to deaths during the heat dome. Sadly, with climate change the number of extreme-heat events is expected to continue to increase.

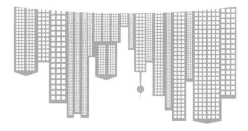

The use of solar panels can reduce greenhouse gas emissions, helping to mitigate the effects of climate change.
LEOPATRIZI/GETTY IMAGES

Ask someone who hangs their laundry outside and they will tell you that doing so makes their clothes smell great and makes their whites whiter.
MICHAEL H/GETTY IMAGES

Reefs like these act as natural barriers against storms. Wetlands, such as mangrove forests and marshes, also play a role in protecting coastal areas.
KIERAN STONE/GETTY IMAGES

Make sure first that your municipality allows it (and if not, write to them and tell them why they should).

- **Compost.** Composting is the process of decomposition that turns organic matter (like food scraps and dried leaves) into nutrient-rich soil that can be used for gardening. It's something you can do on your own at home with food waste, but some municipalities have workers who come and collect this material.

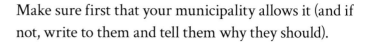

NATURE IS CHANGING

Nature is being affected by our rapidly warming climate. Rising temperatures affect nature in countless ways, including:

- changes in the timing and length of growing seasons
- changes in the migration patterns of animals
- changes in where species can live (which can mean more **invasive** species and pests in areas they didn't inhabit before)
- rising sea levels
- more extreme weather events

In addition to helping fight climate change, we must also work to adapt to our changing world. Once again, incorporating nature can help. Chinese researchers came up with the idea of ***sponge cities.*** These are urban areas with features that help soak up excess rainwater and prevent flooding, such as specially designed green spaces with water-loving plants and ponds.

Coral reefs can also help in adapting to climate change. Protecting and restoring them can reduce the height and energy of large waves. Healthy reefs help protect shorelines and communities that are located near the water.

NATURE SPOTLIGHT: *The Butterflyway Project*

Jordan-Anne Rich of Almonte, Ontario, and Clara Misener of Perth, Ontario, are Butterflyway Rangers for the David Suzuki Foundation's Butterflyway Project. The project is one example of nature-based ***activism*** that helps improve our communities too. Rich and Misener planted "pollinator patches"—small gardens filled with native plants that attract and support pollinators like butterflies—around their cities. They also hosted a plant drive and fundraised to buy soil and plants for community gardens.

According to Rich, there are many benefits to a project like this. It helps the environment by creating habitat for pollinators, and it also deepens our connection with nature and the community. Misener agrees. She says being involved in the project has taught her new skills and helped her make a difference in her community.

Rich and Misener want young people to know that they too can take on community-based projects. "You don't have to worry about being cool or following trends," Misener explains. "Do what you love and know that you're doing great work by helping to protect the environment."

Rich agrees. "Connect with your passion," she says. "Apply what you love to an initiative that helps to make a difference."

Volunteering as a ***citizen scientist*** can be a fun way to connect with nature while doing real science for organizations, governments or universities. Projects could include identifying birds in your neighborhood or testing water quality. There are tons of different projects to get involved in!

Jordan-Anne Rich and Clara Misener are passionate about improving their communities and protecting pollinators.
(LEFT) JORDAN-ANNE RICH; (RIGHT) STEPHEN MISENER

Let's Live with Nature

Is there a place in nature that you feel particularly connected to? It could be in your backyard or in a nearby park. Try to visit it on a regular basis and notice how it changes through the year, as the weather and seasons change.
RADNATT/GETTY IMAGES

Whether through personal hobbies or school activities, we can deepen our relationship with nature in our everyday lives. In this chapter we will explore some of the ways in which you (and your friends and family too!) can get in on the outdoor fun.

NATURE PLAY

There are countless ways to "play" in nature. And don't be fooled—playing in nature isn't just for little kids. Tweens, teens and, yes, grown-ups too can all benefit from unstructured play in the great outdoors. Here are a few ideas of activities to help inspire you:

- Gather wildflowers and press them to use for decorations or crafts later.
- Build a toy boat out of sticks and float it down a creek.
- Lie down and gaze at the clouds. Or stay up late and gaze at the stars!
- Choose a plant that inspires you. Draw or sketch it.

- Design a "fairy house" near a tree or tree stump, using materials like stones and flowers.
- Build a fort out of fallen branches.
- Create a **nature mandala**, a series of circles surrounding a central point, made with found materials such as seashells, stones, leaves or flowers. (The concept of the mandala comes mainly from Hinduism and Buddhism.)
- Pretend you're a little kid again and splash in puddles.
- Skip stones at a local beach or creek.
- Play in the winter—build a snowman, make snow angels, have a snowball fight or build a snow fort.
- Have a scavenger hunt with your friends. See who can find all the plants, animals or items on your list.
- Make nature-based crafts, like hanging flower garlands or leaf prints.
- Do nothing at all! Sit down, feel the soft moss under your fingers, take a deep breath and simply enjoy the moment. This is sometimes called *grounding*.

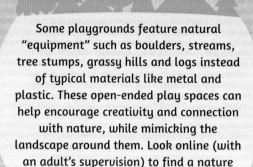

Some playgrounds feature natural "equipment" such as boulders, streams, tree stumps, grassy hills and logs instead of typical materials like metal and plastic. These open-ended play spaces can help encourage creativity and connection with nature, while mimicking the landscape around them. Look online (with an adult's supervision) to find a nature playground near you!

NATURE HOBBIES

Take it a step further with some nature-inspired hobbies or clubs to try. Whether organized through your school, your local community center or an organization, there are many fun ways to nurture your connection with nature. And the best part? These activities can help connect you with like-minded kids who have similar interests.

Here are a few ideas to consider.

- Volunteer at a local environmental organization, doing outdoor activities like removing invasive plants or cleaning up litter.
- Join a photography club and take photos of nature.
- Learn tai chi (which is often practiced outdoors).

The "fairy house" you build doesn't need to be fancy—just use what's on the ground nearby. You'll create a little bit of magic and spread joy for children (and adults!) who discover it later.

JUSTAHOBBYMOMMY/GETTY IMAGES

35

Is there a new skill you've always wanted to learn? Consider doing an outdoor day camp in the summer or over spring break.
JAZALAYYIN/GETTY IMAGES

One example of a typical activity at a nature school: students from EPIC Learning Centre collect and examine fungi.
LINDSAY COULTER

- Join a climbing club for kids or teens.
- Get involved with a local organization for young birders (more on that later in this chapter!).
- Learn how to go trail riding on your bike.
- Join the outdoor club at your school. If one doesn't exist, gather some friends and ask your teachers to start one!
- Take your fitness outside with activities like kayaking, canoeing, hiking, stand-up paddleboarding or horseback riding.
- Take a course on orienteering or survival skills.
- Learn how to garden (many community centers offer courses).

NATURE SCHOOL

Take a moment to imagine a classroom. Do you picture a room with desks and chairs? At **nature schools** around the world, classrooms can be forests, tide pools, meadows and much more. While outdoor education has existed in different forms and different cultures for a very long time, nature schools began in the 1950s in Denmark and Sweden, and are newer to North America.

These schools offer kids an opportunity to learn outside, where they can connect with the land and learn new skills. For example, they can involve exploration in local parks, green spaces (like forests and beaches) or urban or rural (like farms) settings.

EPIC Learning Centre is one example of a nature school. Based in the city of Victoria, British Columbia, EPIC is a registered nonprofit organization and public school with a mixed model of at-home learning and outdoor learning. Writer, educator and naturalist Lindsay Coulter is an EPIC co-founder and former director. At EPIC, "nature is the classroom, teacher and healer," Coulter explains.

Nature school isn't taking traditional academics outdoors. Instead, EPIC's model is about hands-on learning. "We support learners to connect to themselves, one another and the living world," says Coulter.

EPIC also aspires to recognize and include Indigenous perspectives and ways of knowing by incorporating the *First Peoples Principles of Learning* in the daily school experiences. For example, kids see that learning involves patience and time, that it is part of memory, history and story, and that it supports the well-being of self, family, community, the land, the spirits and the ancestors.

Some examples of EPIC student projects include:

- apple-tree *grafting* (with the help of a local farmer)
- horsemanship (how to take care of horses, as well as communication with horses)
- wool processing (including spinning and dyeing it)
- nature restoration (such as pulling invasive English ivy and then weaving baskets from it)
- boat building (using real tools like saws)

If you're interested in attending a nature school, you can research online to see if there is one available in your area. If not, there are plenty of other opportunities for nature-based learning.

- Read the websites of local Indigenous communities to see if they offer events, cultural and historic sightseeing tours, programs or mentorship opportunities for young people.
- Find out what sorts of programs or events are offered through your municipality or local nonprofit organizations. You might find opportunities to go on guided nature walks or remove invasive plants during the summer or on spring break.
- Look for opportunities to incorporate outdoor education at school. Ask your teacher about possibilities for nature-based field trips or class projects. For example, could you collect and test water from local creeks for science class?

What's that flower called again? If you (like so many of us) don't know all the names of the plants in your area, consider using an app for help when you're out on a nature adventure. Many plant-identification apps are available for download on smartphones (with an adult's supervision). Simply snap a photo, and the app will help you identify the plant.

EPIC co-founder and former director Lindsay Coulter loves spending time outside. One of her outdoor activities is horseback riding.
LINDSAY COULTER

Did you hear that? Nature is filled with beautiful sounds. Some people like going on **soundwalks**, which are walks with the goal of listening to nature. Next time you go for a walk in nature, consider making it a soundwalk and listen for sounds like a babbling stream or birds chirping. As you stroll, take in the calming sounds around you and enjoy.

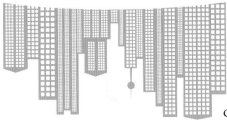

Nature is beautiful all year long, and we can find joy in every season. Consider celebrating seasonal changes by observing the spring equinox, the summer solstice, the fall equinox and the winter solstice.
CATHERINE MCQUEEN/GETTY IMAGES

Land-Based Education

Another example of outdoor education is Indigenous **land-based education** (also known as land-based learning). It's rooted in traditional Indigenous knowledge of nature and the land, which has been passed down by Elders for thousands of years. Land-based education is especially important because this process was almost lost during **colonization**. At that time, Indigenous children were forcibly separated from their families and sent to residential schools, where their cultural practices were not allowed.

John Harris (whom we met in chapter 1) supports land-based education for students in his school district. Activities he and his students have participated in include fishing, crabbing and digging for clams. On these days Harris shares stories and knowledge about the land, so the students learn much more than just the activity that they are doing. "It's a holistic form of learning," he says. "It's learning with spirit. The land is a powerful teacher."

PREPARE FOR NATURE

Need some great gear for outdoor exploration? Dressing for the outdoors isn't just about fashion—proper clothing can help us stay safe and comfortable. Depending on the season and the weather, consider these items:

- rain boots, raincoat, umbrella and rain hat
- hiking boots
- snowsuit (or winter coat and snow pants)
- scarf, winter hat, waterproof gloves and warm socks
- wide-brimmed hat, sunscreen, sunglasses and UV-protective clothing (dressing in layers that are easy to add or remove prepares you for changes in the weather)
- water bottle
- safety gear such as a whistle, compass and map

- nature-exploration gear such as binoculars or a nature journal

Don't worry if you don't have everything! You can slowly build your collection. Consider borrowing items or purchasing them secondhand. You can find great gear at secondhand stores or from such online groups as Swap and Shop or Buy Nothing. (Ask an adult's permission before online shopping.)

RESPECT NATURE

Staying safe and respecting nature are essential parts of enjoying the great outdoors. Have an adult supervise you or give permission before you head off into nature. Always let someone know where you are going and when you will be home, and never hike alone. Here are some important tips for your outing.

- Dress for the weather and bring any equipment you might need. Choose gear appropriate for the time of year, your activity and how long you will be gone. Always bring food and water.
- Know your area. Find out if there are any poisonous plants to watch out for, what the terrain is like (how uneven it might be, for example) and how to navigate an encounter with a wild animal (like a bear or a coyote).
- Stick to the planned route—do not venture off trails or out-of-bounds.
- Find out if there are ticks in your area and how to identify them.
- Be aware of any local rules (such as not starting fires in parks or on beaches).
- Never leave garbage behind—take everything that you brought with you when you leave.
- Don't disturb wildlife.

Bonfires can be awesome! They're not always allowed, though, for safety reasons. It's important to research rules ahead of time in order to have safe, respectful and fun outdoor adventures.
PAMELAJOEMCFARLANE/GETTY IMAGES

Interested in trying birding? Check to see if your local library has a "birding backpack" you can borrow. Many public libraries offer backpacks loaded with birdwatching gear, such as binoculars and bird-identification guides, so outdoor enthusiasts can try their hand at birding. (And if they don't offer this, consider suggesting it to the librarians!)

Now that you're equipped with tools for connecting with the outside world, ask yourself if there's anything you want to take further. If there is a topic you're interested in pursuing, research local organizations or ask your school or community librarian.

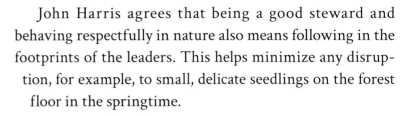

John Harris agrees that being a good steward and behaving respectfully in nature also means following in the footprints of the leaders. This helps minimize any disruption, for example, to small, delicate seedlings on the forest floor in the springtime.

YOUR BACKYARD...AND BEYOND!

There are countless benefits to connecting with nature and many ways that people can get involved, from **birding** to nature restoration.

We can also work to make the outdoors inclusive for everyone and find ways to improve our communities so that everyone can benefit from nature equally. In our everyday lives we can take simple actions to help locally. Here's an example:

- Look at who has access to green spaces like parks and trees, and who tends to have less access. Does your municipality keep data on where green space is located?
- Find out which areas of your city may be subject to extreme heat (or other consequences of climate change, such as flooding). Who lives there?
- Write emails to your local politicians about these environmental and social issues. Ask your local elected officials if they have plans to increase tree density or make your city more resilient to climate change.

Our natural world is a beautiful place, and one that humans deserve to feel connected to. By strengthening our relationship with nature, we can learn how to take care of the environment and how to let the environment take care of us too. Connecting with our incredible natural world is something that we can start right away and continue for our entire lives. So what are we waiting for? Let's go outside!

Harry Sedin
JOHANNA SEDIN

Anica Gorlick
ANDREW GORLICK

NATURE SPOTLIGHT: *Young Birders*

Anica Gorlick, Lukas Miller, Harry Sedin and Clay Zhou-Radies are teenagers who participate in the BC Young Birders Program. They are part of a growing number of young people who have become involved in birding in recent years. These young birders are adapting the activity to make it their own, using things like social media apps. These can be important tools for birders, helping to connect like-minded young people and giving them a place to chat about birding and share their birding photographs.

Birding doesn't require fancy equipment, and it can even be done in cities. All it takes is some curiosity, patience and time. "Jump right into it!" says Gorlick. "The joy of being a birder is something only people who do something they really enjoy know about."

Sedin describes the excitement of finally seeing a bird you've been hoping to see. "Those are the special moments, when you feel fully immersed in nature," he says.

"Anyone can do it," says Miller. "Just start by getting outside, spending time in nature and listening."

Zhou-Radies adds, "Spend as much time outdoors as possible, even in an urban environment. Dedicate a portion of your life to being outside and observing."

Lukas Miller
BIRDSANDBIRDYS

Clay Zhou-Radies
YUAN ZHOU

Acknowledgments

I am so thankful to have had the opportunity to write this book. *Get Outside!* celebrates the natural world and our innate connection with nature, so it's imperative to first acknowledge that I live and work on the unceded Traditional Lands of the Squamish (Sḵwx̱wú7mesh Úxwumixw), Tsleil-Waututh (səlilwətaɬ) and Musqueam (xʷməθkʷəy̓əm) Nations. They are the original stewards of these lands. I am grateful to be able to live, work and play here, and to have the opportunity to act as a steward for these lands.

Thank you to my amazing editor, Kirstie Hudson, and everyone at Orca Book Publishers for your guidance and support throughout the entire publishing process.

My utmost gratitude goes to everyone I interviewed when researching and writing this book. Thank you to Lindsay Coulter, John Harris, Judith Kasiama, Melissa Lem and Linda Åkeson McGurk for sharing your experiences and expertise with me. Thank you to the young birders I spoke to (Anica Gorlick, Lukas Miller, Harry Sedin and Clay Zhou-Radies), as well as Melissa Hafting, who runs the BC Young Birders Program and helped coordinate the interviews. Thank you to Jordan-Anne Rich and Clara Misener, the Butterflyway Rangers I spoke to, as well as Jode Roberts from the David Suzuki Foundation, who helped coordinate the interviews. It is such a pleasure and an honor to speak to and learn from so many knowledgeable and inspiring people. Thank you also to Melissa Lem and Sarah Robertson-Barnes, who acted as expert readers for this book.

Finally, thank you once again to my incredible family for their support and help through this entire process. In many ways it feels as if they wrote this book too. I appreciate every home-cooked meal and every bit of childcare that helped make this book possible.

Thank you, everyone!

Resources

Print

Andrews, Kim. *Exploring Nature Activity Book for Kids: 50 Creative Projects to Spark Curiosity in the Outdoors.* Rockridge Press, 2019.

Clendenan, Megan, and Kim Ryall Woolcock. *Design Like Nature: Biomimicry for a Healthy Planet.* Orca Book Publishers, 2021.

Franklin, Devon. *Put on Your Owl Eyes: Open Your Senses & Discover Nature's Secrets; Mapping, Tracking & Journaling Activities.* Storey Publishing, 2019.

Hoare, Ben. *The Wonders of Nature.* DK Children, 2019.

Mulder, Michelle. *Going Wild: Helping Nature Thrive in Cities.* Orca Book Publishers, 2018.

Rouse, Dan. *The Children's Book of Birdwatching.* DK Children, 2023.

Wohlleben, Peter. *Can You Hear The Trees Talking? Discovering the Hidden Life of the Forest.* Greystone Kids, 2019.

Online

Audubon: audubon.org

Birds Canada: birdscanada.org

Canadian Wildlife Federation: cwf-fcf.org

Child & Nature Alliance: childnature.ca

Children & Nature Network: childrenandnature.org

Colour the Trails: colourthetrails.com

David Suzuki Foundation: davidsuzuki.org

Diversify Outdoors: diversifyoutdoors.com

Intersectional Environmentalist: intersectionalenvironmentalist.com

KidsGardening: kidsgardening.org

National Wildlife Federation: nwf.org

Nature Canada: naturecanada.ca

Nature Conservancy of Canada: natureconservancy.ca

Nature Kids BC: naturekidsbc.ca

PaRx: parkprescriptions.ca

Glossary

activism—the practice of taking action to create change, such as writing letters or protesting

Age of Enlightenment—a movement in 17th- and 18th-century Europe that valued rational thought and science

biodiversity—the variety of life all around us, often measured by the number of different species that exist in a particular area

biomimicry—the practice of using nature to inspire design and innovation

birder—someone who studies birds in their natural habitats

birding—the practice of studying birds in their natural habitats

Black Birders Week—a week-long series of events created by Black birders to celebrate the work being done by Black birders and nature enthusiasts and also bring attention to the discrimination Black people face in the outdoors

citizen scientist—a person without scientific training who participates in scientific projects led by governments and organizations

climate change—the long-term changes in worldwide temperatures and weather patterns

colonization—the act of sending people to settle in another area and subjugating the local peoples (such as Europeans settling in the Americas, even though the Americas were already populated by Indigenous Peoples)

compost—(verb) the breaking down of organic material by microorganisms and other decomposers to create nutrient-rich humus (which itself is sometimes referred to as compost)

conservation movement—the movement to manage and protect natural resources, which emerged in the mid-19th to the early 20th century in the United States

environmental racism—discrimination in environmental policies and decision-making based on race, particularly in terms of which people end up most negatively affected by environmental problems like pollution and climate change

environmental stewardship—the act of responsibly using, caring for and protecting the environment

First Peoples Principles of Learning—learning principles articulated by Indigenous Elders, scholars and knowledge keepers. These principles are generalized and do not represent one particular Indigenous community.

fossil fuels—nonrenewable fuels (materials used to produce energy), such as coal, oil and natural gas, that are formed over millions of years by plant or animal remains

friluftsliv—a Nordic expression, which translates to "open-air living" in English, that describes the importance and joy of spending time outside

geothermal energy—a form of renewable energy generated from heat deep within the earth's core

grafting—joining two plants together into a single plant, which is one way to grow a tree

green spaces—areas of vegetation, such as parks and forests

hydropower—a form of renewable energy generated from moving water

Industrial Revolution—a period of development in the 18th and 19th centuries in Europe and North America that shifted society away from farming and toward the mass production of goods and energy

intersectional environmentalism—environmentalism that includes social issues and examines how environmental topics overlap with and relate to (intersect) other important topics, like ethnicity and gender; rooted in the theory of intersectionality developed by scholar and writer Kimberlé Crenshaw

invasive—(referring to invasive species) plants or insects that arrived from elsewhere and have a harmful effect on their new ecosystem, spreading quickly and making it challenging for native species to thrive

land-based education—(also known as *land-based learning*) a form of education rooted in Traditional Indigenous Knowledge that involves learning from the land

light pollution—outdoor artificial light that is disruptive to humans and wildlife

mariculture—the farming of marine organisms in their natural environments

nature-deficit disorder—a phrase coined by Richard Louv to describe how people, particularly children, are adversely affected by spending too little time in nature

nature mandala—a series of circles around a central point, made with found materials like seashells, stones, leaves or flowers (inspired by mandalas from spiritual traditions, mainly Hinduism and Buddhism)

nature restoration—(also referred to as *ecological restoration*) the practice of working to repair a site in nature after it has been disturbed or harmed (such as by invasive species, a fire or logging)

nature schools—(also referred to as *forest schools*) programs of education that take place outdoors and philosophically value nature-based learning

noise pollution—unwanted and disturbing sound, like traffic

pollinators—animals such as bees and butterflies that carry pollen from the male part of a flower to the female part of a flower (either in the same flower or in a different one), allowing the plants to reproduce

renewable energy—energy from natural sources that can be replenished by nature faster than it is consumed (in contrast to fossil fuels)

resources—materials or possessions that are valuable and useful

rural—of or relating to the country

solar power—a form of renewable energy generated from the sun

soundwalks—nature walks in which you focus on sounds to help you connect with the environment

sponge cities—places with specially designed features that help soak up excess rainwater and prevent flooding, using drainage technology as well as nature

tree canopy—the amount of ground that is shaded by trees; also known as *tree cover* or *tree canopy cover*

tree inequity—a form of environmental injustice in which some neighborhoods have fewer trees than others, which has health and societal consequences

urban—of or relating to a city

urban heat island effect—the tendency of cities to absorb and re-emit the sun's heat, making them hotter than surrounding rural areas or green spaces, which re-emit less heat

wind power—a form of renewable energy generated from moving air

Index

LEAH PAYNE is a writer, editor and mother. She holds a bachelor's degree in communication from Simon Fraser University and a master's degree in library and information studies (MLIS) from the University of British Columbia. She is also the author of *Less Is More: Join the Low-Waste Movement*, also in the Orca Footprints series. Leah lives in Vancouver, British Columbia, where she loves spending time in nature with her family.